# LOST TRAMWAYS OF WALES
# NORTH WALES

## PETER WALLER

GRAFFEG

# CONTENTS

# INTRODUCTION

Although there had been street tramways in Britain from the early 1860s in places like Birkenhead and London, it was not until the 1870 Tramways Act that a legislative framework was established for their construction and operation. The Act empowered local authorities to grant licences to companies to operate tramways for a 21-year period. The licensee could construct the tramway itself or the route could be constructed by the local authority and leased as part of the franchise to the operator. Initially, it was expected that private companies would always operate the tramways built; however, in 1883, Huddersfield Corporation in the West Riding of Yorkshire, having constructed a new steam tramway to serve the town, was unable to find a licensee willing to take on operation and so became the first municipal operator of trams within the British Isles.

The 1870 Act imposed a number of restrictions upon the tramway builder and operator; with the benefit of hindsight, it can be seen that these had a negative impact upon tramway development in the United Kingdom and undoubtedly represented one factor in the demise of the tramcar from the 1920s onwards. One of these clauses required the builder and operator of the tramway to maintain the public highway to a distance of 18 inches outside each running line; this effectively made the tramway owner responsible for the upkeep of the road surface on those streets where trams operated. At a time when the condition of the public highway was often poor, the well-built and well-maintained section over which the trams operated became a magnet for other road users. As road traffic increased, so trams – despite the fact that the road had been constructed to accommodate them – were increasingly perceived as a cause of road traffic delays.

The second weakness within the 1870 Act was the so-called 'scrap iron clause'; this permitted the licensor – usually the local authority – to take over the assets (such as the trams) owned by the licensee at asset value – including depreciation – rather than reflecting the value of the business. As a result, tramway licensees became increasingly unwilling to invest in their business as the licence period came towards its end. The Act permitted the termination of the licence after 21 years and every seven years thereafter. For company-owned operations this sword of Damocles meant that the threat of municipalisation was ever present and, even if never exercised, was sufficient to ensure that modernisation might never take place. The classic example here is the tramways of Bristol; operated throughout their career by a company but with the constant threat of take-over by Bristol Corporation, the system survived through until 1941 operating open-top and unvestibuled trams that would not have been out of place on the first electric tramways built at the end of the 19th century, whereas other systems were operating state-of-the-art modern trams by World War II.

This volume is one of a series that covers the tramways of Wales. It should be noted that, in terms of place names, the book deals with an era when the English spelling was to the fore; this was reflected in the company names, for example, and these historic names have been retained where appropriate. Contemporary spelling has been adopted where the names feature as part of the narrative except for places like Cardiff, Newport and Swansea, where the traditional spelling has been retained as being the most familiar.

## Llandudno & Colwyn Bay

As the 19th century drew towards its close, there was a considerable growth in the popularity of north Wales for holidaymakers and day trippers, with the result that the resorts of Llandudno and Colwyn Bay both experienced considerable growth during the period. Although there was a railway line – the main line from Chester to Holyhead – Llandudno itself was served by a branch off the main line and so there was pressure to try and improve transport connections between the two resorts.

## Origins

On 2 June 1899 the Llandudno & Colwyn Bay Light Railway Order was made; this permitted the construction of a line between the two towns. There were grander plans – to extend to Rhyl and Prestatyn – but these were never completed. However, delays in construction meant that a further order – the Llandudno & Colwyn Bay (Deviation) Order – was obtained on 26 September 1903; this allowed for a half-mile deviation to the original line and a longer time period to construct the line. Contracts for the work were let in 1904 but by 1 May 1905, the stipulated date of completion, little had been achieved. Financial problems led to the project being taken over by a second company – the Llandudno & Colwyn Bay Electric Traction Co; this too, however, failed and was replaced by a third company – the Llandudno & District Electric Tramways Construction Co. Ltd – in July 1907. In the background, work on the 3ft 6in-gauge line's construction was progressing and, following the Board of Trade inspection on 26 September 1907 and the borrowing of two trams, limited public services commenced on 19 October 1907. The full service from West Shore in Llandudno to Rhos-on-Sea, where the depot was located, commenced the following month.

For the line's opening, 14 42-seat single-deck trams were supplied by the Shrewsbury-based Midland Railway Carriage & Wagon Co Ltd; these were supplemented by four single-deck semi-convertible trams, Nos 15-18, supplied by the United Electric Car Co Ltd of Preston two years later.

On 7 June 1908 the line was extended from Rhos to Station Road in Colwyn Bay. Although powers for further extensions were obtained in 1907 and 1912, only a short extension – from Station Road to the Queen's Hotel in Old Colwyn was actually constructed; this opened on 26 March 1915. In 1917 the line suffered its first abandonment when a short section of line along West Parade in Llandudno was abandoned and the equipment recovered for reuse. This section was part of an original planned route to serve Deganwy station that was never constructed. Also during World War I powers were obtained to operate double-deck trams, but these were not used until the mid-1930s.

### Development after World War I
After the war, the fleet was further supplemented in 1920 by the purchase of four single-deck toastrack trams, Nos 19-22, supplied by English Electric. The 1920s represented a difficult period for the tramway as it was an era of unregulated bus competition and, although the tramway invested significantly in doubling most of its route between 1912 and 1931, the section east of Colwyn Bay suffered from severe bus competition. As a result, the section from Greenfield Road in Colwyn Bay to Old Colwyn was abandoned on 21 September 1930.

The tram was in retreat in many towns and cities across the UK and the Llandudno & Colwyn Bay took advantage of this to acquire second-hand trams from Accrington, Nos 1-5 in 1932, and from Bournemouth, Nos 6-15, in 1936; this allowed for the withdrawal of all bar seven of the original fleet. The ex-Bournemouth trams were to be the first double-deck trams operated by the company.

### World War II
During World War II the 7 ½-mile tramway played an important role transporting many of the staff of those government departments transferred to north Wales. In 1943, however, part of the route at Penrhyn Bay was seriously damaged as a result of high tides and gales; this was not the first time

that this had happened – damage had previously occurred in 1927 and 1933 – and the same was to happen in October 1945. On all these occasions, however, the damage was repaired. The next time – during the winter of 1952/53 – that this occurred, the decision was made not to repair all the damage but to operate the section as single track. The company was afraid that the grants made by the government to the council to fund improved sea defences might result in the loss of tolls that it derived from road traffic.

**After World War II**
In late 1945 the tramway fleet was to be reduced by one, as No 16, one of the surviving original trams, was destroyed by fire. The next year was to witness the last additions to the fleet when two streamlined double-deck trams, Nos 23 and 24, were acquired from Darwen in Lancashire. Following conversion from 4ft 0in to 3ft 6in, the two were put into use on shuttles either in Llandudno or in Colwyn Bay. Unfortunately, the company's hopes of using them on the entire route were dashed by the Ministry of Transport following an inspection in 1948; the Ministry refused to allow them in public operation over the steeply graded section around Little Orme. The company also undertook significant work on track replacement during the immediate post-war years but, if this seemed to indicate a long-term future, this was an illusion.

After the war, passenger traffic declined, falling almost 50,000 between 1953 and 1954 and, despite a fares increase in the summer of 1953, losses were increasing. The board started to consider the future of the tramway; the perceived threat to the line galvanised efforts by its supporters to try and preserve it – after all, railway preservationists had secured the Talyllyn Railway earlier in the decade – but these hopes came to nothing. In late 1955 the company obtained its first buses, but the closure was not straightforward. The Traffic Commissioners for the North West decreed that a joint timetable with Crosville, the company that operated most local bus services, had to be agreed before conversion could follow.

In the event, the tramway's final demise was precipitated by an unexpected source: the Manchester & North Western Electricity Board (MANWEB). Historically, the tramway had bought its power from local power stations; the nationalisation of the power industry under the Electricity Act of 1947 changed this relationship. MANWEB recalculated the costs involved in supplying the tramway and announced that the tramway's existing contract would not be renewed after the summer of 1956. MANWEB was prepared to continue supplying the line, but at the prohibitive cost of £100 per day. The board had no option: it decided to abandon the tramway. The last services operated on 24 March 1956. The last tram to enter the depot early on Sunday 25 March was No 8. After closure, the fleet – with the exception of one of the ex-Bournemouth trams that was preserved – was scrapped at Rhos, whilst the tramway itself was dismantled.

The company continued to operate buses for a further five years before selling out to the much bigger Crosville company.

## Great Orme Tramway

Although the Llandudno & Colwyn Bay was the only electric tramway serving Llandudno, there was and is a second tramway in the town – the Great Orme Tramway. Although fitted with overhead for much of its life and thus giving the appearance of being an electric tramway, the two sections of the Great Orme Tramway are in fact powered by cable and, given that the two tramcars on each section are permanently linked to the cable, the tramway is more correctly to be regarded as a funicular.

It was in 1898 that Great Orme Tramways Act was passed; this permitted the construction of a single line from Llandudno to the summit of Great Orme and authorised the company to raise £25,000 to fund the construction. Before work started, however, it was decided to split the line into two sections (a lower section of 872yd and an upper of 827yd), in all totalling just over a mile in length, and adopt the 3ft 6in gauge.

By 1900 all the necessary land had been acquired and by March the following year over £21,000 of the required funding had been raised. Construction started in April 1901 and, although there were some problems, testing of the lower section commenced on 23 May 1902. This section opened to the public on 31 July 1902, following the formal inspection the day before. The upper section was inspected formally on 8 May 1903; the inspectors were not happy, however, and required further work to be completed before a second – successful – inspection on 7 July 1903. Having been approved, public service on the upper section commenced the next day without any formal ceremony. The average gradient for the lower section is 1 in 6½ – with a maximum of 1 in 4 – and that for the upper is 1 in 15½. The two sections meet at Halfway, where the original power house was situated. This was equipped with coke-fired boilers to power the winding gear

for the two cables used, one on each section.

When new, the line was provided with three freight vans – Nos 1-3 – and four passenger cars: Nos 4 and 5 for the lower section and Nos 6 and 7 for the upper. The freight cars were supplied for the movement of goods and parcels, as stipulated in the original Act, but were also used for the carriage of coffins from the town for burial at the church on Great Orme. The freight wagons, which could either be propelled up the gradient by being pushed by one of the passenger cars or attached independently to the cable in lieu of a passenger car, were all taken out of service by 1911.

The line, having opened, was to have some 30 years of relative success; however, on 23 August 1932, passenger tram No 4 was to be involved in a fatal accident when its drawbar failed. In the resulting crash, the tram driver and a 12-year-old girl were killed and 10 other passengers were seriously injured. The Inspector's report into the accident, issued the following year, was highly critical of the tramway, highlighting the fact that the emergency brake was inoperative at the time of the accident and that the drawbar's manufacture – from a steel alloy – was unsuitable for this type of use.

In February 1933 the company held its AGM, at which it was reported that the tramway did not have a reserve fund nor was the insurance cover adequate to settle the claims resulting from the accident. As a result of the latter, the local Sheriff took possession of the line on 7 June 1933 and, on the same day, the board decided to petition the High Court to seek the compulsory winding up of the company. This Order was made on 24 July 1933; however, at the creditors' meeting that resulted from this, held on 25 August 1933, it was decided to try and sell the line as a going concern.

Following the successful conclusion of brake tests, the line reopened on 27 May 1934 and, in December the same year, was sold to a new syndicate; this was to become known as the Great Orme Railway Ltd in March 1935. It was only in 1977 that the line reverted to using 'Tramway' in its title. In 1947, Llandudno Council, using powers enshrined in the 1898 Act, decided to purchase the tramway. As a result of a disagreement over price, the council exercised its powers of compulsory purchase in November 1948, backdated to 31 March 1948 and effective from 1 January 1949. With its main asset now in council ownership, the Great Orme Railway Ltd was wound up in 1950.

Under council ownership, there were some changes; of these the most significant was in 1957 when electricity replaced the coke-fired boilers that powered the two cables. It was estimated at the time that the change would save more than £1,400 per annum. The livery has also undergone several changes, although this largely affects the shade of blue in which the four passenger cars are painted. In 1965 a brick passenger shelter was constructed at Halfway, whilst in 1991, as a result of a new radio communication system, the overhead – which was only required for communication purposes between the drivers of the two trams on each section – was removed, although the trams retained their trolleypoles for aesthetic reasons.

Today, the tramway, now owned by Conwy County Borough Council, continues to ply its way between the town and the summit of Great Orme, carrying over 200,000 passengers annually. It is the UK's only surviving street cable tramway (or funicular) and the only operational tramway of any form in Wales. From 1999 onwards the line underwent a £4.5 million upgrade, partly funded by the European Union and by the Heritage Lottery Fund, as well as the council; this resulted in a new interchange station at Halfway and other improvements.

### Other tramways in north Wales

North-west Wales was the home to four small horse tramways. Pwllheli possessed two of these. The older of the two was the Pwllheli & Llanbedrog. This started life as a 3ft 0in-gauge mineral line constructed by Solomon Andrews as he sought to develop the town as a holiday resort.

The mineral line opened in 1893 and connected West End, in Pwllheli, to a quarry 2½ miles away at Carreg-y-Defaid. The primary purpose of the line was to carry stone for use in the construction of the town's sea wall. The line was extended into the town centre during May 1894 and passenger services commenced that summer. Eventually, in 1898, the passenger service reached Llanbedrog – Andrews had recently acquired the Llanbedrog estate – resulting in a single route that ran for just under four miles. A number of horse trams – including the three used by the corporation on its own line until 1920 – were utilised, all painted in a dark red livery.

One of the weaknesses of the line was that it was largely constructed in the sand dunes, with the result that it was often damaged by stormy weather. In 1896 the original alignment was lost and the line was rebuilt slightly further inland. However, on 28 October 1927 a tidal storm surge saw the sea encroach significantly inland and destroy much of the tram route.

Lacking the resources to restore the tramway, the owners offered it to the corporation. The offer was declined however, and the tramway subsequently abandoned.

Alongside the Pwllheli & Llanbedrog, Pwllheli Corporation operated a short – ½-mile – route linking the town centre and railway station with the beach. The line, believed to be 2ft 6in in gauge, opened on 24 July 1899. To operate the route the Shrewsbury-based Midland Railway Carriage & Wagon Co Ltd supplied three trams – two open and one enclosed – painted in a blue and white livery. The service survived until the summer of 1920, when it ceased at the end of the season. The three trams passed to the Pwllheli & Llanbedrog. Some years after that line closed, the body of one of the corporation-owned trams was salvaged for preservation and restored.

To the south of Pwllheli, there was a short-lived horse tramway that served the town of Harlech. Little is known of the line and there are no known photographs of it. However, it is shown on maps and extended to three-quarters of a mile. The gauge is believed to have been 2ft 0in. The line opened in July 1878 and closed about five years later.

Across the Mawddach estuary lies Fairbourne; this is now the home of the miniature Fairbourne Railway. However, when the line was originally constructed, it was a 2ft 0in-gauge horse tramway that linked Fairbourne to Penrhyn Point Ferry. The line originally opened in 1895, primarily for the shipment of construction goods. It was sold in 1911 and, five years later, the new owners decided to convert the route to 15in gauge; it was converted to 12¼in gauge in 1986.

**Glyn Valley Tramway**
There was one other horse-operated passenger line in north Wales; this was the Glyn Valley Tramway that ran west from Chirk up the River Ceiriog valley to Glyn Ceiriog and Hendre. This was both a passenger and mineral line. Originally proposed as a standard-gauge line in the 1860s, the new company was incorporated

as the Glyn Valley Tramway by an Act of 1870. The line, built to a gauge of 2ft 4½in, was completed in 1873, with the first horse-powered passenger services operating on 1 April 1874. In 1885 powers were obtained to divert the line at its eastern end to serve Chirk station, to extend the line beyond Glyn Ceiriog to serve the quarries around Hendre and to upgrade the line to permit steam operation. In order to allow the work to be undertaken, passenger services ceased on 31 March 1886. Although steam-operated freight traffic commenced in 1888, it was not until 15 March 1891 that passenger services were reinstated to Glyn Ceiriog. These were to survive through until 6 April 1933, when competition from a recently introduced bus service through the valley led to their withdrawal. Freight traffic continued for a few years but this too ceased; the line was closed in July 1935 and subsequently dismantled.

**Wrexham**

Apart from Llandudno & Colwyn Bay, the only other electric tramway in north Wales served Wrexham. It was in 1874 that the Wrexham District Tramways Co was established; the company obtained powers to construct a 3ft 0in-gauge horse tramway from the town southwards to Ruabon – a distance of five miles. In reality, only the section between Wrexham and Johnstown was completed; this opened using a sole tram on 1 November 1876. A second open-top double-deck tram, built by Starbuck of Birkenhead, was soon added to the fleet. Initially the services were poor but, in June 1884, a local inn-keeper, Fred Jones, took over the lease and added a third, locally-built tram, similar to that supplied earlier by Starbuck. The fleet of three trams sufficed for the duration of the horse operation. Ownership of the line – but not the operation – passed to the Drake & Gorham Electric Power & Traction Co in 1898; the new owners announced that they planned to electrify and extend the system, although Jones continued to operate the line in the interim. Before the new owners could act on their plans, for which they had received powers in 1899, the company was acquired in 1900 by British Electric Traction and a new company – Wrexham & District Electric Traction Co Ltd – was set up as a BET subsidiary.

In 1901 the new owners gained further powers for the extension and electrification of the line; in order for the work to be undertaken, the horse trams operated for the last time on 26 April 1901. The route was operated by horse buses whilst work on the tram route was completed.

For the new electric trams, the gauge of the line was widened to 3ft 6in and a short extension was added towards Ruabon; as with the original company, however, the ambitious plans of the new owners for a network of routes was never fulfilled. The first electric trams operated on 4 April 1903, with the system eventually extending to almost 4½ route miles. The main service operated from Johnstown through to a terminus on Mold Road, through Wrexham town centre, along with a short branch from Johnstown to Gardden Lane; this was a distance along the authorised route to Rhosllanerchrugog (Rhos) which was never completed. To operate the

service, 10 open-top double-deck trams were supplied by Brush of Loughborough; painted in a deep red and cream livery, these were the only trams ever owned by the company.

Rather than develop the tramway to cope with expanding demand, the company introduced its first buses prior to World War I and, reflecting the changed nature of its operations, the company name was changed to the Wrexham & District Transport Co Ltd in 1914. By the 1920s the tramway was in need of significant investment but the company decided to replace it with buses; following a slow run-down, the last trams operated on 31 March 1927. A number of derelict tram bodies survived with the result that, although not preserved at the time, two have been salvaged and are currently in an unrestored condition.

### A note on the photographs
The majority of the illustrations in this book have been drawn from the collection of the Online Transport Archive, a UK-registered charity that

was set up to accommodate collections put together by transport enthusiasts who wished to see their precious images secured for the long-term. Further information about the archive can be found at: www.onlinetransportarchive.org or email secretary@onlinetransportarchive.org.

Great Orme
Summit

Halfway

Llandudno

Clifton
Road

Grand Theatre

Penrhyn Hill

Maes Gwyn Road

West Shore

Rhos-on-Sea

Colwyn Bay

Old Colwyn

The only depot used by the Llandudno & Colwyn Bay Electric Railway was situated on Penrhyn Avenue in Rhos-on-Sea. Constructed in timber on a steel frame, the depot opened with the trams on 19 October 1907. Following the cessation of tram operation in March 1956, the company used the building as a bus depot until 1961. After use for commercial purposes, the depot was subsequently demolished. Here ex-Bournemouth car No 8 is pictured outside the building.

The interior of one of No 17; this was one of the three cars that dated originally to 1907 which survived post-war. It had been No 14 when new.

The upper deck of one of the ex-Bournemouth cars, No 8.

The two ex-Darwen cars were the most
modern to operate on the Llandudno
& Colwyn Bay; this is the upper deck
of No 24.

GWALIA WALLPAPER
CHAPEL ST · LLANDU

12

Following the closure of the short section to
West Shore, the terminus of the L&CBER was
at the western end of Gloddaeth Avenue.
Ex-Bournemouth No 12 awaits departure
from the later West Shore terminus.

Heading eastwards is No 2 en route to Colwyn Bay; it has just passed No 11 en route to the later West Shore terminus at the Clifton Road passing loop on the approach to the terminus.

At the eastern end of Gloddaeth Avenue, before the tramway turned into Mostyn Street, the route passed the Palladium Theatre. Although probably designed before World War I, the theatre was not completed until 1920. This Grade II listed building is still extant. It no longer functions as a theatre, having been reopened as a pub in 2001. Ex-Bournemouth No 8 is pictured passing the theatre as it turns into Mostyn Street. Note the duty inspector who controlled movements at Palladium Corner, especially on busy days when 'extras' terminated here from Colwyn Bay. The company relied heavily on the summer trade when the trams were often packed with holidaymakers but, in inclement weather, the competing buses were often preferred.

On the corner of Mostyn Street and Gloddaeth Avenue is the Carlton Buffet pub; this is still extant. Unfortunately that is no longer true of ex-Bournemouth

No 11 pictured as it turns into Gloddaeth Avenue heading for West Shore.

With Great Orme in the background, No 11 – one of the 14 single-deck cars supplied for the line's opening in 1907 – heads into Mostyn Street from Gloddaeth Avenue. No 11 was one of four of the batch to survive after World War II, being renumbered 18 in 1936.

Another of the first batch of trams is pictured heading westwards along Mostyn Street towards Gloddaeth Avenue. Although much of the track through Llandudno was doubled between 1912 and 1931, there remained a short section of single track at this location through to the line's closure in 1956.

Situated at the western end of Mostyn Avenue is the Grand Theatre; this Grade II* listed structure was completed in 1901. It was to remain a theatre until 1985 before being used as a nightclub. After a brief period of disuse, it reopened as a nightclub in 2016. Here one of the post-war survivors from the original fleet, No 18, heads eastwards to Colwyn Bay past the striking red brick theatre.

# BODAFON FIELDS

Having passed to the south of Llandudno Bay along Mostyn Street, Mostyn Broadway and Mostyn Avenue, the tramway entered a section of private right of way across Bodafon Fields. With the summit of the Orme in the background, ex-Bournemouth No 8 is seen heading east.

With the sea beyond the village of Penrhynside, No 3, in the fleet's original pre-World War I livery of maroon and cream, descends towards Llandudno. The sign in the field beyond – 'Building land to be sold' – is indicative of changes that were to come. In the century since this view was taken, both sides of Bryn Y Bia Road have seen significant development, with new houses constructed.

# PENRYHN HILL

One of the original batch of trams, No 11 (renumbered 18 in 1936), heads up the gradient towards the summit of Penryhn Hill. At the time of the photograph, this section was still single track; it was later to be doubled.

Having just passed the summit on Penryhn Hill, toastrack No 19 has crossed the B5115 and is descending towards Penrhyn Bay. The driver has the white summer top on his cap. By the date of this photograph, these trams were the last totally open toastracks in operation in the UK. Always popular in good weather, those on board would often smile and wave to passers-by and people on the trams heading in the opposite direction. The conductor collected the fares by walking along the outside running board; here, however, he is in position ready to ensure that the trolley does not leave the overhead during the steep 1 in 11 descent. The toastracks were only used during the summer months and so were retired during 1955.

One of the four English Electric-built
toastrack cars, No 21, descends
Penrhyn Hill as it makes its way
east towards Colwyn Bay.

Ex-Accrington No 4 heads towards Colwyn Bay having stopped at the Little Orme Café stop at the bottom of Penrhyn Hill.

Passengers for Colwyn Bay were
provided with this small shelter at the
Little Orme Café stop.

# MARINE ROAD

The section of line at Penrhyn Bay was subject to the threat of coastal erosion. Although damage was incurred in both 1943 and 1945, it was over the winter of 1952/53 that the most severe erosion occurred, with the seaward line being lost. Although there were efforts made to underpin the line and improve the sea defences, it would have proved too costly to complete the work, with the result that part of the section along Marine Road was to remain single track through to closure. One of the ex-Bournemouth cars, No 8, is seen during an enthusiasts' tour with the erosion clearly evident below it.

This is the section along Marine Road following the singling of the line after the damage inflicted on the tramway over the winter of 1952/53. This was a toll road owned by the tramway company; the proposed improved sea defences would potentially result in the company losing much of its toll income.

# RHOS-ON-SEA

Ex-Bournemouth double-deck No 13 heads towards Colwyn Bay along the Promenade at Rhos-on-Sea.

With the pier at Rhos-on-Sea in the background, No 8 – one of the original batch of cars supplied in 1907 (and one of the 10 withdrawn in the 1930s) – heads from the Esplanade into Whitehall Road. The 1,300ft-long pier was opened originally in 1895. Damaged by fire, it was finally dismantled in 1954.

Although the bulk of the route from Colwyn Bay to Llandudno town centre was double track, the short section over the ex-London & North Western Railway, Chester to Holyhead main line at Brompton Bridge was single. Here toastrack No 21 is seen crossing the bridge en route to Colwyn Bay.

# COLWYN BAY

In Colwyn Bay, between Coed Pella Road and Woodland Road West along Conway Road, there was a short section of interlaced track; here one of the original cars that survived post-war, No 17, heads east towards Colwyn Bay over this section.

Passengers board ex-Bournemouth double-deck tram No 8 outside St Paul's church in Colwyn Bay prior to making the journey towards Llandudno. Apart from the tram and a more recent casualty – the local branch of Woolworth (now replaced by a Spar) – this scene is very similar today as virtually every building is still extant.

Standing at the post-1930 terminus in Colwyn Bay is ex-Bournemouth No 7.

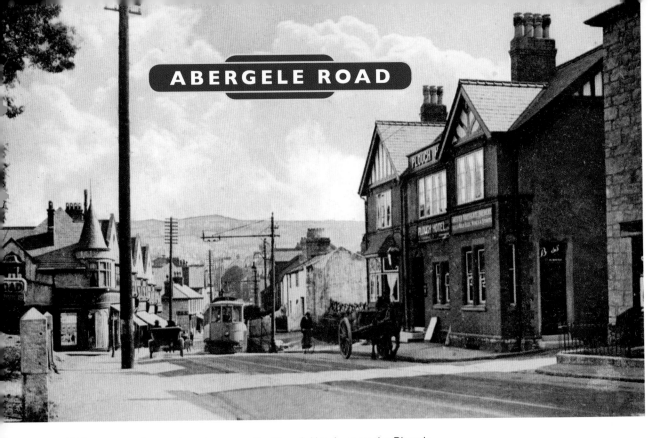

# ABERGELE ROAD

In 1915, an extension eastwards from Station Road, Colwyn Bay, to the Queen's Hotel, Old Colwyn was opened along Abergele Road. With the Plough Hotel – now the Plough Inn – in the foreground, one of the original batch of single-deck trams heads west towards Colwyn Bay.

A second view of the short-lived section along Abergele Road sees No 8 approaching the junction of Berthes Road with Abergele Road in Old Colwyn, heading toward Colwyn Bay. Although there are now no trams along this road – the Colwyn Bay to Old Colwyn section closed on 21 September 1930 – the majority of the buildings recorded in this view are still extant, with the exception of the terrace on the extreme right.

# THE END

Exit pursued by a bike: on the last day of operation – 24 March 1956 – ex-Accrington No 4 is pictured passing Maesgwyn Road on its way back to Llandudno with a cyclist in hot pursuit.

The sad sight after the closure of the
line in March 1956; one of the ex-
Bournemouth trams is dismantled in
the depot yard at Rhos.

**GREAT ORME**

Great Orme No 4 stands in the Llandudno terminus of the lower section of the Great Orme Tramway; this was the tram that ran away in the fatal accident in 1932 that almost resulted in the line's closure in 1933.

The two lower-section trams pass on the loop on Ty-Gwyn Road. The Great Orme Tramway is more properly a funicular, with the trams counter-balanced, rather than a normal cable tramway where the cars can operate independently. Thus the passing loop is situated exactly halfway between the town centre terminus and Halfway, where the upper and lower sections of the tramway meet.

In early July 1950, one of the two trams that operated the upper section, No 6, stands outside the shed at Halfway.

The same day, No 6 is pictured again, this time at the Summit. Although fitted with overhead and with conventional trolleypoles – thus giving an impression that the line is powered by electricity – the overhead and poles were in fact used for communication purposes between the crews of the trams on each section. It has subsequently been removed.

**PWLLHELI**

A view of the Pwllheli & Llanbedrog tramway at the southern end of West End Parade in Pwllheli; the line heading inland at this point is towards the railway station whilst the line's depot was situated slightly further to the south.

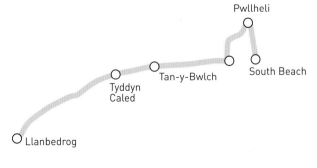

Pwllheli

South Beach

Tan-y-Bwlch

Tyddyn Caled

Llanbedrog

A view of the Pwllheli & Llanbedrog looking southwards along West End Parade in Pwllheli; the proximity of the line to the coast is evident.

Further north the line ran through the dunes and damage from the sea resulted eventually in the tramway's final closure.

Pwlheli Corporation operated three single-deck horse-drawn trams – two open and one closed – all supplied by the Shrewsbury-based Midland Railway Carriage & Wagon Co Ltd. This was the fully enclosed car and is seen in the fleet's blue and white livery. All three passed to the Pwllheli & Llanbedrog in 1920 and, following rescue, the enclosed car was eventually preserved and restored.

Between opening and 1916, the Fairbourne was a 2ft 0in gauge horse tramway; this view, looking towards Barmouth across the estuary, was taken towards the end of the period. The postcard was franked on 24 August 1915.

**GLYN VALLEY**

One of the four steam locomotives operated by the Glyn Valley Tramway – No 2 *Sir Theodore* – is pictured with a mixed train at Chirk station. The 0-4-2T locomotive was built by Beyer Peacock in Manchester and was new in 1888; loaned to the Snailbeach Railway in Shropshire for a period in 1905, the locomotive was scrapped following the closure of the Glyn Valley in 1936.

**WREXHAM**

The Wrexham & District Electric Tramways Ltd possessed two depots. There was one in Johnstown that originated with the earlier horse tramways but was rebuilt for the opening of the new electric service in 1903. It survived until the system's closure in 1927. A second – short-lived – depot existed on Maesgwyn Road in Wrexham between 1920 and 1925. This view, taken in 1904, shows the interior of the Johnstown depot.

Mold Road○

Wrexham ○

○ Rhostyllen

Gutter
Hill ○   ○ Johnstown

○ Bangor Road

The Wrexham fleet comprised 10 open-top double-deck trams all supplied by Brush for the line's opening. One of the fleet is pictured in Regent Street, Wrexham. The livery adopted by Wrexham & District was deep red and cream.

# CREDITS

Lost Tramways of Wales –
North Wales
Published in Great Britain in 2018
by Graffeg Limited

Written by Peter Waller copyright © 2018.
Designed and produced by Graffeg
Limited copyright © 2018

Graffeg Limited, 24 Stradey Park
Business Centre, Mwrwg Road,
Llangennech, Llanelli, Carmarthenshire
SA14 8YP Wales UK  Tel 01554 824000
www.graffeg.com

Peter Waller is hereby identified as the
author of this work in accordance with
section 77 of the Copyrights, Designs and
Patents Act 1988.

A CIP Catalogue record for this book is
available from the British Library.

ISBN 9781912213139

1 2 3 4 5 6 7 8 9

## Photo credits

© Phil Tatt/Online Transport Archive:
page 16, 19, 20, 22, 25, 26, 30, 33, 35, 37,
38, 39, 40, 43, 51, 52, 53.

© R. W. A. Jones/Online Transport
Archive: pages 18, 21, 29, 44, 47.

© Barry Cross Collection/Online
Transport Archive: pages 27, 28, 31, 32,
42, 46, 48, 49, 56, 57, 58, 59, 60, 61, 62.

© F. E. J. Ward/Online Transport Archive:
pages 36, 50.

© Peter N. Williams/Online Transport
Archive: pages 54, 55.

**Cover:** Llandudno.

**Back cover:** Pwllheli, Gloddaeth Avenue,
Wrexham.

**Lost Tramways of Wales series:**

- **Cardiff**
  ISBN 9781912213122

- **North Wales**
  ISBN 9781912213139

- **South Wales and Valleys**
  ISBN 9781912213146

- **Swansea and Mumbles**
  ISBN 9781912213153

**Lost Tramways of England series:**
Autumn 2018: Coventry, Bristol,
Nottingham and Southampton.